# *a* WALK *in*
# HER SHOES

# a WALK in HER SHOES

## REFLECTIONS OF A MOTHER AND DAUGHTER ABOUT LIFE

YEWANDE AND TOMISIN OGUNNUBI

Copyright ©2018 Yewande & Tomisin Ogunnubi

ISBN: 978-978-55613-9-5

All rights reserved.

No part of this book may be reproduced, distributed, stored in a retrieval system, or transmitted, in any form or by any means, electronic, electrostatic, magnetic tape, mechanical, photocopying, recording, or otherwise without prior written permission from the Authors or Publisher.

For information about permission to reproduce selections from this book, write to info@wrr.ng or yewande.ogunnubi@gmail.com.

National Library of Nigeria Cataloguing-in-Publication Data

Layout & Cover Design by: Nancycovers

Printed and Published in Nigeria by:
Words Rhymes & Rhythm Limited
Suite C309, Global Plaza Plot 366, Obafemi Awolowo Way, Jabi District, Abuja, Nigeria.
08169027757, 08060109295
www.wrr.ng

# CONTENTS

ACKNOWLEDGEMENT . . . . . . . . . . . . . . . . . . . . . . . . . . . . . iii

PROLOGUE. . . . . . . . . . . . . . . . . . . . . . . . . . . . . . . . . . . . . . . . v

**CHAPTER ONE**
Friends and Foes . . . . . . . . . . . . . . . . . . . . . . . . . . . . . . . . . 1

**CHAPTER TWO**
Body Image and Fashion . . . . . . . . . . . . . . . . . . . . . . . . . . 6

**CHAPTER THREE**
Spiritual Matters . . . . . . . . . . . . . . . . . . . . . . . . . . . . . . . 14

**CHAPTER FOUR**
Of Sexuality, Predators and Deceivers . . . . . . . . . . . . . . . . . . 20

**CHAPTER FIVE**
Values and Inspiration . . . . . . . . . . . . . . . . . . . . . . . . . . . . 28

**CHAPTER SIX**
The Boy-Friend Thingy . . . . . . . . . . . . . . . . . . . . . . . . . . . . 36

**CHAPTER SEVEN**
Navigating the pain valleys . . . . . . . . . . . . . . . . . . . . . . . . . 45

**CHAPTER EIGHT**
Discipline versus Punishment . . . . . . . . . . . . . . . . . . . . . . . 53

**CHAPTER NINE**
Gratitude Mode . . . . . . . . . . . . . . . . . . . . . . . . . . . . . . . . 58

**EPILOGUE**. . . . . . . . . . . . . . . . . . . . . . . . . . . . . . . . . . . . . 64

**CONVERSATION STARTER: CHECKLIST** . . . . . . . . . . . . . 67

*In memory of Damilola Abokede Obinna. You were a mother in every sense of the word; you poured your all into many girls.*

*The void remains…..*

# DEAR DAUGHTER

Thus far, recriminations.
Over the years, scarifications.
Through it all, discriminations.

I carry them in my lashes, looking down
always in submission.
I carry them in my tongue twisting
when I so desperately want to defend myself.
I carry them in where I am allowed to go,
and when I am allowed to go.
I carry them in my inability to count the coins of my hard labour.

I have wondered many times; is this all?
I have searched the meaning of life and asked,
"Is this all?"
I have tasted bile and guile thinking, 'Is this all?'

Then you came, dear daughter.
It was a mixed feeling of fear and hope.
You came through my pain;
My pain of limited opportunities,
My pain of failed expectations,
My pain of rejection and abuse,
My pain of forced union,
And my travail of nonentity.

As I sat in the corner of my sparse life,
I had many dreams.
I dreamt of days when I will have freedom to choose.
I dreamt of a time when I will wake without trembling.
I dreamt of people and places I wish I knew.
I dreamt of a life different from the one I have.

Dear daughter, now that you are here,
I will dream through you.
I will teach you what they refused to teach me.
I will show you what was hidden from me.
I will love you with an affection I never experienced.
I will push you on, and not pull you back like I was.

Oh! How I dream...
Though afraid and unsure, my dreams for you are many.
I dream that you will rule your world;
whichever one you desire to build for yourself.
I dream that you will be unstoppable;
whatever height you set your sights on.
I dream that you will be unforgettable; making your mark in the world through your gifts and talents.
I dream that you will be free; not conforming to any standard but yours. Standards you have set for yourself by reason of knowledge and wisdom.
I dream that you will be happy;
whatever happiness means for you.
I dream that you will be fulfilled;
emptying yourself before you leave this world.
My hope for you is that you believe in yourself much more than I believe in you.

Dear daughter, you are my dream; now I will live through you.

- *Yewande Ogunnubi*

# FOREWORD

I am highly honoured to have the co-author, Yewande and Tomisin, of this very valuable and unique book, request that I write a foreword for this Reflections of a Mother and Daughter about life, titled "A WALK IN HER SHOES", through a mutual friend of ours.

Reading through the nine (9), chapters and the interesting life stories and conversations between mother and daughter, sharing their experiences and relationships between the 'nurturer and nurtured', It clearly gives us the perspective of how our children view our generation and vice versa but also outlines the invaluable role of women in building strong human beings as we inculcate in them core values such as caring, civility, cultural values, decency, discipline, empathy, moral servitude and life skills.

Turning the pages of this book, it reads like an autobiography because of the simple writing and many truths I agreed with.

We must at all costs play our part as responsible adults, guardians and parents, in contributing our part into nation building and raising well-meaning and good mannered individuals.

Our children must be allowed to dream, make their marks in the world, set standards of their own, and above all, be encouraged to leave positive footprints. We all must endeavour to pass on the baton, have successors and leave this world empty. (My sayings that I found written in the book).

We must not compromise our standards because we do not want to upset our children. Rather, we should be firm as we instill values, the fear of God and respect for all irrespective of class or creed.

However, we must allow our children their freedom of expression, ability to be honest and maintain openness to approach us whenever necessary while we correct them in love.

This book is highly recommended for all ages, race or nationality and everyone who is interested in developing an effective and positive parenting style.

I congratulate Yewande and Tomisin Ogunnubi for this giant stride.

*Best regards*

**Abimbola Fashola (Dame)**

*Chairman, LEARN/ELLA CARES*

## ACKNOWLEDGEMENT

Our sincere thanks and gratitude goes to God for designing our lives as is. We have no doubt that he planned that we will write this book from the foundations of the world.

And then he graced us with these two unbelievable boys to keep us sane and 'insane' all in one lifetime. Thank you Adeyinka and Daniel, we love you.

Our gratitude also goes to Mrs. Abimbola Fashola for taking out time to read and write the foreword. Your life and work inspires. Thank you Bukky Shonibare for your thoughts and input. Thank you Mrs. Rhoda Ayinde for your encouraging words.

To all our real life and adopted aunts and uncles...even on social media, we are grateful that you are always taking the front roll in cheering us on.

# PROLOGUE

## MOTHER

Hers was a pregnancy that scared me. Her daddy might even say, "It was a pregnancy I did not want." I won't describe it as unwanted, though. But it just didn't fit into my plans. I had my perfect plan of how the first three years of my marriage would pan out. I had planned for no kids until after two years (for educational reasons). Then between her dad's and doctor's gimmicks, my plan was not backed up with sufficient knowledge of how to SERIOUSLY prevent pregnancy. Suffice to say, she came when I was not expecting her.

And then the desires for ambitious things took over my appetite. Craving for hard pawpaw was insatiable, and next was desire for moi-moi (steamed bean pudding) and eko (corn meal). Those were delicacies a Yoruba girl living in the South South of Nigeria could not easily find. That should have been a sign that this little one would hold no prisoners in her quest for greatness.

Then the 'hardship' she endured for almost 9 months in the womb; from momentous time in 'molue' buses in unending traffic in Lagos, to plenty cold in the country of birth. She survived it all. She survived the lack too, and became the epitome of resilience from day one.

She was not an instant hit with her mom. The bond that is often touted between a newborn and the birth mother did not happen. It felt like a logical wheel; the typical art of just carrying a load and dropping it. What next? I had asked myself after her birth. Everything was mechanical; from bathing, breastfeeding and rocking her. Until slowly, but surely, she started melting her mother's heart.

Her name pre-empted fate. It was predestined. Her scent filled her world way before she came. The smell of sweet flower, Jasmin. A garden of beauty, attractive in bright colours.

She looked very small. Small, but mighty. She was a mini-me, but a splitting image of her paternal grandma. I knew from that moment that she would represent the old and the new. Her definition of the old and the new is way different from mine, though. Different is good, isn't it?

## DAUGHTER

What is the harm in being different? It is a wonder to me when people say they can't get along because they are 'different'. What fun would anything be if we were all totally the same? We would have no one to counter our views and correct our actions; and there will be no one to look up to since we are all the same. My point is; it is good to be different. Our differences distinguish us from other people, and it makes us unique.

I can't even imagine being the same as my mother. Oh no! There would be no mother-daughter relationship as we know it right now. My mother has always been a storyteller. My earliest memories comprised storytelling moments that made me feel good with lots of laughter. When she was home, in between travels, she was the typical mom. She would wake me up for school with my breakfast prepared and my packed lunch ready. After school, she would help me with homework, comfort me when I was sad, and scold me when I did something wrong. My mom has always been the one I could always go to when I wanted something badly. She is the shoulder to cry on, and also the one whose attention I continuously seek. Up till now, not much has really changed from my childhood.

Where the phrase 'My mother's daughter' may not fully apply to me, I am certain we share a common tendency to 'overthink' things. That tendency is in overdrive mode sometimes. We know. In many other ways, we are very different. Our differences exist for a reason; to help improve and balance us. We need to embrace it. If at all the differences pose a problem, we need to get over it, rather than placing it in the way of a promising relationship.

Plus I had heard countless stories about how things were when my mother was younger. The 'olden days' it is called. I find myself constantly comparing then and now to determine which is better. Personally, I can't imagine living in the generation my mother grew up in, because the way of life was so different from how I know it now. My mother (representing the old school) looks at things from the olden days' perspective, but I believe my generation is better and more interesting. I am obviously biased; in the battle of the new versus the old. I stand with the new way of doing things.

Surely, the old can get along with the new. Being different is good, and finding a common ground is the key.

# CHAPTER ONE

## FRIENDS AND FOES

### MOTHER

My idea of friendship is surely an extension of my personality (which has evolved over time, of course). I am Choleric Sanguine, and so I make friends very easily. I do not like anyone to be uncomfortable when I'm in the room with them, so I will walk up to say, 'Hello'. Not all new 'friends' will stick. I lose many as easily as I make them. Only some glue can keep me connected with new acquaintances. It would mostly be a combination of oozing intelligence, wit, kindness, and an unbridled desire for the simple life.

I love to gist about many things. I am mostly an open book (or so I think), and so love conversations on any subject, including personal ones. I learnt in my generation, though, that there are certain conversations a woman must not publicly engage in. Sorry. I love to have real conversations with my friends, even seemingly uncomfortable ones.

I am for friendships that are about giving. Giving of time and resources to the one you call a friend. Parasitism is a 'no no' for me. There must be something you are bringing to the table. That is how I smell fake friends from real ones. There must be value added in one way or the other. Otherwise, I get tired of such friendships easily, and they will fizzle away after some time.

My definition of friendship is not about uncontrolled emotions all over the place. To act like you own me is to lose me. There is no exclusivity in this business for me. I cannot fully understand people crying over the fact that a friend is not talking to them or shuns them. It is my friend's prerogative to decide who and when they want to talk. I feel I owe them that liberty and they owe me same.

Don't get me wrong, I love it when a friend is loyal, but not to the point where they do not have a life other than what is going on in the friendship. It would suffocate me. Before now, I would sneer at friendships that was full of tears, breakups and makeups. Now, I am more sympathetic. I have a daughter, and I am trying to see everything from a different perspective.

I wish my daughter would just walk up to people she likes and say, 'Hello.' But she would not. Even after many coaching sessions on how to go about it, she would freeze when she gets close to the human target. I don't blame her because she is not me, and she doesn't have a blabbermouth like me. She is not warm, fuzzy and huggy like I am (or pretend to be). She is her own person. She makes and keeps friends in a way suitable to her. I grudgingly accepted that fact as she grew older.

As for foes, I do not think I have them. Enemies? None that I know of. At least, not from my end. I am sure some people dislike me for my outspokenness or my inability to look away in the face of perceived injustice, human rights abuse or unprofessional conduct. I say sorry to them; it is not personal.

I cannot think of anyone whose name pops up in my head and leaves a bitter taste in my mouth. Not now, not ever. I guess I would have moved on, long before such acquaintanceship makes me develop bile. Life is too short; I cannot afford to waste my energy on something unproductive.

## DAUGHTER

Friendship is basically having those people close to you that you can talk to, gist with, and have some level of care for. A friend to me is someone that I can meet with; at least share some kind of personal relationship with.

In a way, I make friends naturally. I am not someone that pushes for friendships, fights for them or work hard to get them. I just get the friends I get. I rarely walk up to people and say the first 'Hi'. But if I find a common ground with someone, for example, we both start to laugh about something or he/she likes something I like, I initiate a conversation. It's easier that way because rather than thinking of what to say, we already have a starting point. I would rather people approach me anyway and strike up a conversation. I most likely won't be the one doing so.

I have a lot of close friends, but not just anyone can cut it. It's not really like I choose my close friends, they just kind of grow on me. I get closer to people when they have certain characteristics like some level of common sense and maturity. I can't stand anyone that can't act sensibly, or one who behaves like a 5-year-old. But amidst the whole maturity thing, I love people with some bit of 'crazy' in them; the good kind. It gets really uninteresting to be around people with boring lives and regular routines. Even the littlest bit of madness would suffice. Then I love when people are willing to be real with me. Yes, we all 'form' a lot of times, but when you still do that on a friend-to-friend basis, Naahhh. I can't be real and open to someone if they aren't the same. One thing that I know my friends and I can never stop doing is talking, talking and talking. I would basically have all types of conversation with my friends, unless it's something I'm really embarrassed about. Most of the time it's either about the people I like or despise, or various stories, or just random things.

My definition of a close friend might be different from others. The fact that we are close doesn't mean we have to do everything together, or we have to dress alike or stuffs like that. We ought to be close to a level where I tell the person things I probably wouldn't tell someone else; where I know the other person almost inside out. All the ideas of sleepovers and 'friends forever' are just unnecessary. We don't have to have planned our future as friends for us to be close, we can be close at that moment and that's all that matters.

I don't really know my mom's friends personally, but I've heard their stories, and I've interacted with some. One thing I admire is that they all share a bond with each other, through thick and thin, and they still remain strong till their adulthood. She knew the kind of friends to keep around her; no one had a negative influence on her. Growing up, I was always told (more like threatened) with the fact that bad friends won't do me any good, and some people even intensified it by saying that such friends would completely destroy my life and all. So I have always checked the kind of friends that I make. Unlike me, my mom is pretty outgoing, and wouldn't even hesitate to walk up to a person and start up a conversation. I would actually love to emulate that attitude, but I don't even bother because I'm just not like that. I can make friends just as easily as I can drop them. I don't know how to accommodate people who don't know the difference between a friendship and a marriage. Some friends are just way too clingy and expect too much from you, and I am definitely not one to put up with that kind of attitude. When our friendship starts becoming too demanding, I won't even hesitate to end it.

Speaking of the people I despise, it takes quite some time for me to despise anyone. If someone has a very foul attitude, behaviour, or habit, and does not want to correct it, that can already piss me off. When that person then shows that foul attitude towards me consistently and continues to act unruly, then I start to dislike the person. If the person resorts to doing something that affects me generally, or does an act that has a negative effect on me, then I start to 'hate' that person. I rarely allow myself to make enemies, but when someone calls for it, I will be more than happy to.

# CHAPTER TWO

## BODY IMAGE AND FASHION

### MOTHER

This is a tricky one. Image of self has evolved over time. Of course, I read the magazines too, and wanted to have all the curvatures of the models featured in them. I guess my practical side came to terms with the reality of being a black African woman; and we mostly have flesh in all the right and wrong places.

I was not so bothered about not having big boobs growing up. The way I thought about it, it saved me the discomfort of wearing a bra. Oh, how I relished the many years of teenage life and early adulthood without the inhibitions of a bra. My 'singlet' was just perfect. I was not afraid of being embarrassed by joggling boobs as I walked to and from school. It was just perfect. I did not think that anything was wrong with me (I also did not think anything was wrong with those who had it in abundance).

I had situations where a male tailor took my measurements for the first time (to sew the remaining one and half yard fabrics pulled from mama's wardrobe) and commented unabashedly on how I had perfect statistics. I responded with a smile. I was pleased with the compliment, and it was good to know. But that was it; it ended there. It did not add any more value to my life than a chilled bottle of coke would after a visit to Yaba market on a very hot afternoon.

There were the other compliments like, "You have lovely eyelashes", "Wow! Your nails look really nice", "I just love the look of your lips; you do not need lipstick at all", "What I would give to have fine legs like yours", etc. They had their place in the scheme of things, and for what it was worth, they often sprang up as a defense mechanism when I came across young ladies who thought themselves beautiful just because they had a string of cash-paying boyfriends. Beyond that, what my body looked like was not my priority. I was more interested in getting compliments on what my sense 'looked' like.

Good for me that my disposition to my body image was not outrageous from the onset. While the beating my body has received in the last few years would make anyone cringe in front of the mirror, I think I am handling it pretty well. I would not be human if I did not have those moments of doubt, worry and shame. I have had them sometimes. Any sane person would have them when they find themselves in the company of some chiseled, handsome bloke. That sudden feeling of regret at wearing the sleeveless top that reveals the flabs in your arms, or the week of tormenting yourself for not committing to that exercise routine. Those moments are worsened when another well contoured, flat-bellied female goddess joins the company. An involuntary intake of breath takes place, and you find yourself sucking your belly in. How long you can keep that belly sucked in without contorting your face in pain is another matter for another day. It happens; I have had my share of unhealthy body image. In some cases, I have responded by doing the needful, from weight loss to body toning through exercise. In other cases, especially for nature/circumstances designed body shape I have no control over, I count my blessings for what I have. It's not easy, but doable when you have no choice in the matter.

I loved and still love fashion just like anyone else. Please note that I refer to my definition of fashion. I have learnt to know what is comfortable for me and what is not. My mood sometimes dictates what I want to wear, and my value system dictates what I eventually wear. I live by that "all things are lawful, but not all things are expedient" standard. In truth, what is expedient has been a moving target. Even at an older age, my mother's stern warning about my choice of clothes is still ringing in my ears. I tried to stick to her standards, but I know I failed sometimes. I am watching my daughter now and wondering how I am doing with the advice on clothes choices. The crop tops scare me, but what do I know? I am old school.

My body image is influenced by the lifestyle choices I make, including the food and drinks I allow into my body. I am aware that I am what I eat. It has been a rollercoaster ride following what I know about weight gain, weight loss, fitness, and what makes for healthy living. I am still on the journey. When I follow the plan, I sense it in the fashion choices I make. When I don't, my fashion sense is haunted.

## DAUGHTER

When people ask me, "What is the best body type?" I'm like, "It's such an obvious answer. The best body type is hourglass!" That is what almost everyone wants. It means you have the figure 8. It is literally a perfect shape. A lot of people are so bent on improving their body type, but I really don't do anything because I doubt there's anything I can do. Sometimes I try to eat to gain weight (if that makes anything better); it never works. I find that some people search for particular exercises that improve their body type. I still don't bother myself; it's just unnecessary stress.

Girls know and are aware of the effect of exercise on their body type. The lazy ones, like me, can't really be bothered to exercise because it's basically way too much stress. But a lot of girls are very enthusiastic about improving their body type and commit to exercise for long hours daily. Some can go to the extent of sacrificing junk food almost every day. Many others know it's healthy to stay off junk food, so they will make an attempt to stay off it, but they will eventually drop the routine.

The truth is, people around me have a strong influence on the image I have of myself. Unknown persons on the internet and media platforms have a way of either improving or downgrading my self-image—mostly downgrading it, though. I find myself constantly wishing I was like someone else, or comparing myself to another. Girls tend to fuss about the body parts they want, and I won't say there is a particular one that all girls fret about. Different people fret about different body parts, but most people just fret about them all. You can't really blame us; everyone wants to have it all.

Sometimes when I look in the mirror, and I don't see the shape I desire, there is a rush of different emotions. First, there's that bit of anger; the one that comes with not getting what you want. Then there's sadness for a while; a feeling of unfairness of some sort, and you will end up beating yourself up for not looking like that girl in your class. Then eventually there's that moment of realisation (with a hint of satisfaction) when you accept that you can't really change anything, so you might just as well enjoy how you are.

People say that no one shape is better than the other, but I believe otherwise. For example, I believe that having an hourglass shape is better than having a rectangular shape!

Come on, nobody wants to be straight in any way. Yes, I get it that body types are different; that there are many people who look better pear-shaped (a person who has hip measurements greater than their bust measurements), and would look odd with an hourglass figure. But in general, some body shapes are way preferable to others.

I have never been embarrassed by my body type, but I have a petite body frame for my age, and people have used that against me at times. It gets to me that because of my small frame, I find myself being compared to people three years younger than I am. Not that I am as bothered as I used to be, but if I had the choice, I would rather have a bigger body frame.

The issue of fashion sense is another problem amongst teenagers. For me personally, I don't have a particular 'fashion sense'. Most times, I wear what I feel comfortable in. Other times I wear what I feel is 'trending' or in vogue, according to what my friends say. My mother usually, if not always, has something 'not too nice' to say about my dress sense. It's either I'm too dressed down in my jeans or my outfit doesn't match, or my shoes are too 'simple', or the dress is too short. Most times she gets her way especially with that 'look' or vibe she gives off when I'm wearing something she doesn't like, but I'd rather just put on what I feel like wearing.

I don't think mothers understand how their daughters feel about their body and choice of fashion, because the need to look good and be seen as 'peng' is higher now in this generation than in theirs. Most moms may feel that, "At her age, it is just to go for birthday parties and put on clothes," but what girls wear is a way of making themselves feel good and socially acceptable. Often, a mother might pick out a certain outfit for her daughter in all innocence. For the fact that the outfit makes her look odd amongst others, she becomes self-conscious. Afraid of what others think of her look, her interaction with others becomes greatly affected.

It's basic; almost every girl wants fine boys to like them, or find them attractive, or cute at least. A girl would most likely dress in a way that would make others, especially boys, to perceive her as fine. If a guy makes a comment about a girl's body or look, it tends to have more effect on her, especially if it is negative. In order to satisfy the guy's standards, the girl may dress in a way that he finds nice and pretty. Sometimes some girls are way too concerned about what boys think that they would go out of their comfort zone. They just 'dress to impress'. No doubt, a line needs to be drawn here.

People are quite judgmental in this day and age. I find that the self-esteem of most girls grow from the number of compliments they receive. Some girls depend too much on compliments to the extent that they would continue to doubt themselves until someone makes that one good comment that makes them feel better. Girls love to be complimented on their fashion sense or at least be assured, even in the slightest way that they don't look like total rubbish. When someone speaks negatively or makes rude, unsavoury comments about my body type, I immediately feel a sharp sting in my chest because it is definitely offensive. I sometimes get self-conscious and accept what has been said as the truth. At that point, I doubt any previous compliments I may have received, and then start to psychoanalyze myself. The moment will pass, though, and I will be back to my confident self.

To boost their daughters' self-confidence, moms should allow them exercise their sense of fashion while monitoring the decency of the fashion sense. They could give them regular compliments on how good they look, at least to make a little difference. Some mothers don't realise that the occasional insults they throw at their daughters have a lasting effect. I feel that moms should allow their daughters do what makes them feel good from time to time, rather than restricting them to their own standards.

# CHAPTER THREE

## SPIRITUAL MATTERS

### MOTHER

Growing up in a Muslim family comes with a lot of responsibility and loads of fun, at least from the mindset of a child. I learnt discipline through the compulsory 30-day fast. We were encouraged to start early. At age ten, I would wake up with others for the midnight meal. Many times, I participated in the cooking of the meal. The fact that I was fasting was a badge I wore very proudly when in school with my mates then. It made me feel more spiritual than those who did not fast. What I did not tell my friends then was that the aroma from their lunch packs was killing me softly. On many occasions, it was torture. On days when my warrior mode could not take it, I snuck sweets, biscuits, oranges, and any other thing I could find in my mouth. I would go home still pretending to be fasting. In those days, the wall clock and sleep were my favourite things during fast. Some days, the clock just refused to move its hands as fast as I wanted it, so I learnt the art of sleeping by force to run down the clock until the call to break the fast was loud and clear.

Fast forward to secondary school days when I had my conversion experience. The memories still gives me the chills. I look back with gratitude for the foundation laid for my Christian journey, howbeit in an atheism touting school. I still reflect that those were the best years of my spiritual quest. The fellowship, the persecutions (I reflect on it now as deserved punishment for disobeying school rules!), the supernatural manifestations, the urgency of soul winning, the ardent study of the Word, and the bond amongst those in the community of faith. It is a nostalgic feeling.

In those days, you would never want to be seen or heard singing secular songs. Even Whitney Houston's 'I believe that children are our future' was not allowed in some quarters. The songs had to sound like a hymn back then to pass the test of how spiritually mature you were. Dan Carman and Helen Baylor were the closest to what those of us who considered ourselves radical Christians could attempt with fast-paced music.

It was an era where you could not think of putting on jeans as a believer. What?! That would be considered a 'far left' action. It was also the period where we debated the spiritual implication of putting on earrings or any bling-bling. The zeal of God's house was so consuming that you avoided being unequally yoked with unbelievers. Those verses of scripture were literally interpreted as meaning you could not consider friendship with anyone other than born-again Christians.

No one necessarily needed to follow anyone up. We went riot with our faith; no holds barred. Every platform was an opportunity to testify. Then, Bible study time was not compromised by buzzing sound of notification from Instagram, Facebook, Snapchat or WhatsApp. The slogan then was 'No Bible, No Breakfast' (NBNB). Now, "Wisdom is the Principal thing" or "Wisdom is profitable to direct" are the more popular scriptures. The perfect scriptural excuse for a less stringent Christian walk, I must say!

The brand of faith being brandished in this generation is slightly different, I think. It seems to be more 'convenient and paced'. There is no sense of urgency. It doesn't seem to affect the clothes worn, the play list on iTunes or the language spoken. I do not hear much of "God bless you", with the 'bless' sounding as 'blesh' to give it a more spiritual intonation. All the young people now speak in tongues mainly through the short hands/emojis used in conversing on social media. Only they and God understands what they are saying; even the devil cannot decode the language, how much more an old school like me. What do I know?

No matter how difficult it is becoming in a very self-seeking world, I know my daughter needs to hold her faith fast to her chest. I tell her how it used to be in my time and how that journey has brought me to this point. I hope she is learning through my actions that her profession of faith must produce good fruits. That the Father seeks those who worship Him in spirit and in truth, and not by spiritual gymnastics.

## DAUGHTER

Humans need God; that is just the fact. Well, the fact I believe in, anyway. A human being should have a solid relationship with God to the extent that it is evident in their lifestyle. We don't depend on God for the sake of it, we do so because we need Him. So, building that relationship is really important. A relationship with God, from my point of view, should be like the one you have with your best friend, just more respectful. It should be one where you put God at the top of all you do and have that daily assurance that there is a mighty being over you.

To be very honest, there is so much going on around me— secular, everyday things —that serves as a major hindrance to the level of my relationship with God. There are those times when I'd pass on reading my Bible because I want to do something else urgently. It is sometimes really hard not to give in to the things around me because it's almost like there are so many 'worldly' things competing for my attention.

I am born again, and I have no doubt about that. My faith experience is mostly because of the influence of my parents. For the fact that I was born into a Godly family, and raised on Christian doctrines, that led to me giving my life to Christ. I had to and wanted to anyway. Faith is actually a really important factor in my life because it is basically what keeps me going. There were so many times when I needed something almost impossible to happen, and I did nothing but held on to my faith, and I had that assurance that it would happen. It always did, and that gave me more reason to stick with God. My Christian faith in general sets boundaries and checks for me so much that there's always that little voice in my head when I'm about to do something totally against my faith, telling me the right thing to do.

Truthfully, I don't see many young people around me serving God. Let me rephrase that; I don't see a lot of young people serve God the way my mother described in her days. They are too engrossed in the 'pleasures' of this world to actually settle down and build a real relationship with God. It's like they have this attitude of 'God will understand'. A lot of young people know about God, but don't really push to know Him on a personal level.

There are some who are actually very close to God, and others who are very far from Him. I say this based on the lifestyles I have observed. In a lot of people's lifestyles, there is no sign of God. It is like young people just live without caring whether they have God to account to. People would rather pretend like God doesn't exist, or God isn't bothered, so that they can just as easily act as they like, without any guilt whatsoever. This is not said to judge anyone or make myself look better than anyone. I am not perfect, and we are all a work-in-progress.

Generally, people criticize young people who profess to be Christians and wear tattered jeans, read romance novels, or listen to secular music. It is common to have young people read all genres of novel or sing along to popular tunes. I agree it may not be completely right for a young Christian girl to follow suit, but we do have to realise that it's not completely wrong either. Not all secular music is 'bad' music. Secular music or 'worldly music' (as sometimes called) include songs with good and uplifting lyrics. The fact that it is not mentioning 'God' should not, and does not, make it bad. Romance novels, in the right context, are not exactly bad because if Christians are allowed to have romance in their lives (I hope we are!), then why shouldn't they be allowed to read about it. Tattered jeans, when done way too over the top, don't always look decent, but if it's ripped in few spots, then there's nothing exposed. I think, therefore, that nothing's really wrong. It's just fashion.

We are young people, and young people want to explore, have fun and mix with everyone. In my view, religious intolerance is not an issue among teenagers. Most people (at least within my circle of friends) don't see you with a label of your religious belief, and it's actually really easy to accept everyone's religion. I am a Christian, and I have Muslim friends; so what? Sometimes we openly talk about the basis of our faith without feeling awkward about it. My best friend could even be a Muslim. It doesn't mean anything to me to be honest, and also it doesn't mean I believe or understand everything about her religion, or that she understands mine. Mutual respect and religious tolerance is what I count as important.

I know that not everyone who claims to be a believer actually is. If the person is a true believer, then his/her lifestyle must correlate to what God has commanded. The person would desire to know God and spare time for God. There would be a level of control that the person would have managing temptations.

My mother relates faith to me in a good way, but I don't see many parents doing that. It comes across like 'believing', or faith is forced down the children's throat. They go like, "You must believe or you're not my child," or "If you don't believe, you will perish in the unquenchable flames of hell," and other scary stuffs like that. And they really expect the children to keep the faith? Wow! The best approach is to use issues that are important to teenagers as case study to show them why they need God and why their faith is important. Tell them the limit they can go with things they do, rather than forcing them not to engage in anything at all. Mothers need to learn to share their thoughts in a relaxed atmosphere, and not 'so serious talk' way of passing the message so that their daughters can understand and think for themselves. When done right, mothers won't need to push their daughters to keep faith; they will do it of their own accord.

There are many role models young Christian girls can emulate. Role models are very useful in motivating us, and they are also useful in clarifying knotty issues. We choose role models for different reasons. Some people follow others because they are in the same sect. Some choose role models because of the good works such people do. I would assume that pastors generally serve as Christian role models. For me, my parents are my role models.

# CHAPTER FOUR

## OF SEXUALITY, PREDATORS AND DECEIVERS

### MOTHER

I cannot remember if I was warned against any awful looking person in my neighbourhood. Sexuality discussions did not seem very common at the time, at least not around me. The few times I heard about the evil that men (I mean mankind plus womankind) do in homes against children was at the hairdressing salons. It was a taboo to even call out my own vagina, how much more refer to another person's. In my time, you are to close your eyes when kissing scenes took place on TV, or pretend that you are disgusted beyond words.

The internet did not mess with our innocence, perhaps because we did not have it. I trusted every neighbour like they were family. I can't remember being warned not to relate with neighbours. I cringe now when I remember times I stopped at a friend's place when walking back from school. I would eat my fill of rice and plantain, and even sleep there for a while before taking the final leg home. I never questioned the motive of the uncle who served me a bottle of coke. I never questioned the spirituality of the uncles and aunts in church who we joined for vigil. I am not even sure my parents wondered for one moment what my fate would be in the home of the family members we had gone to observe a long holiday with.

Going to the pool, I was never afraid of the possibility of being molested under water. What was of concern to me then was not having a fashion faux pas with my swim suit or bikini as available at different times in my growing up years.

I did not suffer abuse in the hands of family members or neighbours. I even thought such did not exist in my time. I have been proven wrong time and time again by the sad experiences of others who did not escape unscathed. Maybe I just enjoyed God's grace and mercy. I was so naïve, and I could have been taken advantage of. I sometimes think, though, that my sharp mouth and my usual Bruce Lee stance must have scared potential predators away. Maybe.

Many things I know about sex and sexuality, I gleaned from Mills and Boons, James Hardley Chase, Pacesetters, and many other series or authors I cannot even remember. I started reading these books as early as age ten. I was a voracious reader. I read mostly for pleasure, to understand why people do what they do; even at that age. But pictures stuck in my head. For a very active mind like mine, I had ideas for experimentation. I did not talk to anyone about it. I would hope that it is not the same for my daughter. I would hope she could ask me anything about everything.

Suffice to say, God shielded me. I don't know what else to attribute it to. But I won't count on the same luck for my daughter. It is better to be safe than sorry. I would rather swallow the misplaced moral and social 'shame' of talking to her about the reality of sex and sexuality, the world view on gender issues, and the high network and net-worth of sexual predators online and offline, than be riddled with guilt of being a careless mother. I would rather be uncomfortable having discussions with her about how she came into the world than having it when she brings another into the world way before she is ready for it.

Just as any mom, my first time of having the sexuality discussion with my daughter was uncomfortable. She was just seven. Her friend was visiting with us at the time. "We were told in school that HIV is contracted through sex. What is sex mum?" The question was popped in church while we waited for her dad after service. Alarm bells went off in my head. What do I say and how do I say it? I knew well enough that telling her fables was not the answer. I bolstered some courage; with a calm demeanour, and I told them we would have the discussion when we got home. And we did. I basically provided information about the functions of the male and female organs, and how God designed that through the reproductive organs, babies would come into the world. The information was as basic as it can get. I let them know that there is only so much they could understand at that age, and that as they grow older, I would make efforts to lay out more information. I provided information I felt was appropriate for her age until she came into puberty. Then, we had to do the menstruation and pregnancy talk! Talking sexuality became easier with each passing mother/daughter moments. The more gist time we had about day to day events, the more opportunities I had to casually throw in sexuality information. I was determined to try my best in this area, and I read up as many books and articles that could help me do a good job.

I believe a mother should not be too liberal in how she verbalizes her disdain for abuse. I am very okay with dropping hints for neighbours, teachers, youth leaders, friends, family that I do not suffer fools gladly when it comes to the issues of abuse, and any form for that matter. I should not even hear that an attempt was made. The colour of my eyes and my skin changes. I know, she knows, and they know. It is my cross and

I really hope I am carrying it well.

## DAUGHTER

If adults are in doubt, they should now know that young people do talk about sex and sexuality. Most of the time it is not a serious, deep talk. It is just in a jocular way.

I don't feel odd or weird when people discuss sexuality issues around me; neither do my peers. Truth be told, it is something I am used to hearing. Information, both genuine and fake, land on our laps through different medium. Teenagers have different preference for the source of sexuality information. Some might prefer to learn about it from their parents, while others might feel weird talking to their parents about it. There is that feeling that being parents, they would probably go into 'serious' mode and give that straight face, followed by, "I think it's time, dear, for us to have THE TALK." And then for girls, it will most likely end with the hit line: "Close your legs!" To be frank, I think the majority of teenagers would really prefer to have such conversations with their peers because, obviously, they'll just joke around while hitting the points.

Fortunately or unfortunately, I got my first batch of information from my mom. (I don't think my dad was supposed to hear this story, but, oh well, too late). So after being brainwashed and blatantly lied to all my naïve and innocent childhood life that babies came as a stalk from heaven (story books), or as a gift from God (church), the truth finally came to light. There was the usual half-truth from over-zealous elders that, "If a boy touched you, wham! You're pregnant'. That was my case when I slept on the same bed with my little male cousin one day, and an aunt who lived with us told me I could get pregnant. I was almost in tears fearing I might have gotten pregnant until my mom intervened. When my mom laid with me and decided to tell the unbelievable story of how things actually worked, how pregnancy occurs, and how babies are brought to life, Lord knows I felt like I had been given the craziest, and might I say, disgusting news ever. I can still remember my wide-eyed self, trying to take in the crazy information. Honestly, I still didn't believe much of what she said at the time, and I preferred to live on with the earlier fairy tales. My school then began sexuality education on a lighter note, and well, I grew up.

In fairness, adults are always eager to make sure young people have sufficient information to protect them from predators. We have been baptised with countless talks, lessons and advice that I can confidently say we know a lot. However, I'm not really sure a lot of young people take as much precaution as advised. If I could use my friends and me as a case study, we know what is out there and we know how to protect ourselves to an extent, but you never know when you are being unnecessarily over-careful or not careful at all. The fact that there is constant news of rape and acts of sexual violence may inhibit some young people from living their lives to the fullest, but the majority really just go on with life with the attitude of 'Well, nothing has happened to me'.

With regards to young people's attitude to predators and deceivers, there are three categories of young persons. First, the ones who chain themselves up with the fear of falling into the hands of predators, and fail to live normal lives. Secondly, the ones who gain awareness from information like this, and use it to guide and protect themselves while living a normal life. Then the others who don't have a care in the world, and go on living like nothing changed. I think people should go for the second because there's really no reason to completely reroute your life when a little adjustment is what is necessary. One thing I know is that young people in general are reckless. That factor may be one of the major things leading to abuse. There's usually this air of nonchalance, like we must have fun

24/7 before we die, and then we don't take the necessary precautions to protect ourselves. It might just be those things that make us susceptible to abuse sometimes. I am well aware that there are some people with depraved minds, who are bent on abusing young people, no matter how careful they are. I hope law enforcement can help deal with them.

The risk of abuse on social media is another area of concern. It is on the high side at the moment, with lots of young people falling prey, but it is nothing that cannot be prevented. Young people need to understand the broadness of social media. They should stop posting while believing it is only seen by their friends. They should stop posting things that reveal personal information. They should not post seductive pictures or information that draws predators toward them, and they should definitely not trust everybody that reaches out to them.

Mothers do have a role to play in protecting their daughters from different types of abuse. First, they must not be abusive themselves, otherwise their daughters will accept abuse as a norm. Secondly, I think teaching them a defence mechanism is key. Obviously, teenage girls need to know how to take precaution, but also need to know quick action steps to take should they find themselves in an unexpected/bad situation. They are likely to feel less helpless when they know they can fight for themselves, rather than waiting for someone else to save them.

Mothers who have daughters that have fallen prey to abusers have a role to play in helping them. Incidents like that are very traumatizing, and the agony rubs off on the mother too. For starters, they can help them move on, because dwelling on what's done would not change anything. It is not the time to rain insults on the girl or blame her for what happened. I think mothers have the primary role of helping them get past it by encouraging them and giving them guidance on next steps.

As for me, regarding 'sexual relations' with a boy, I have set my boundaries. Even when I had not, the boundaries have been pre-set for me by my parents. The fact that I know that the set rules and limitations are for my benefit, it gives me courage and confidence to keep these values, and live according to them.

# CHAPTER FIVE

## VALUES AND INSPIRATION

### MOTHER

If there is any value that I am so sure emerged from the home front living with my mom and dad, brothers and sisters, it was the fact that you were not at liberty to use the words 'Oloshi', 'Oloriburuku', 'Were', etc. Or common abusive Yoruba words, literally meaning, 'You are mad', were never used at home. In fact, I remember thinking that my father was some sort of 'Americanah'. He spoke so fast, and mostly in English. To entertain the use of such foul language was demeaning for me, even as a young girl.

I do remember episodes in the public primary school I attended, when classmates would meet to fight at the end of school periods, and during the fight, foul words would be brandished, in different shades. But no matter the extent of my anger at any one in school then, I felt it was beneath me to even mention those words. They were so heavy for my mouth to call out. It felt so uncouth, so bush. Even milder comments like, "Your head is not correct," never sat well on my tongue, because they were not words/phrases/language used at home.

Dad was (still is) a stickler for honesty, hard work and community service. He had a bad reputation (in a good way) for calling people out for stealing public or community resources. He frowned at ostentatious living, even though he could comfortably afford that lifestyle in monetary terms. An example of that was on my wedding day. I rode in my dad's almost ten- year old Volkswagen Santana car to the church. He would never be a party to borrowing a jeep or fancy car that was not his own just to impress anyone.

There were those painful moments when dad would travel out of the country (he travelled for business a lot), and you would do a list of clothes and other fancies for him to buy, but he would tell you, without batting an eyelid, that the same clothes can be bought for cheaper in-country. It was no fun to meet him up at the airport in those days, because there was nothing to look forward to. As his kids, we did not even entertain any hope of candies when we saw him wheel more than one travelling bag through Immigration. Even the corrupt Immigration Officers were always disappointed. When asked to open his bags for inspection, all they will find would be plenty books. An Immigration Officer once asked him if he was a professor of some sorts. They just could not understand how this 'regular customer' through immigration was not in possession of contrabands.

And when you talk about achieving everything only on merit; that was dug into my skull from early on. Dad will tell you that he has never begged anyone for school admission, and he was not going to start with any of us, his kids. He would tell us, "If you value your education, you will sit, read and pass your exams convincingly. And then you will obtain school admission by merit. But if you do not pass, I have no inhibitions about you repeating the exams until you pass."

There was no 'platter of gold' with him. Lack of necessities was never an excuse because he provided everything humanly possible to make us thrive. The rule was that the other part of the equation to achieve success rested in our hands.

I learnt from my mom that altercations was not becoming of a well-bred lady. Not once did I see her exchange words, even when we lived in an apartment; sharing a compound with people from different backgrounds and walks of life. With mom, I experienced a true life depiction of long-suffering; a staying power that was admirable and worth emulating. What I cannot say for certain is whether I have successfully added that value to my repertoire. I know for certain that I do not like suffering at all. Who does? From my experience in raising her, I know my daughter too cannot endure suffering. Perhaps, she needs to spend more time with her grandma. It may be too late for me, but for whatever it is worth, I know I learnt resilience along the way. Long suffering is still a long thing.

And when you talk about humility, it's a non-negotiable virtue in my household when growing up. It was not just talk; it was actioned. It was a case of "there is nothing that we have that we have not been given". And that virtue extended to mean we must cultivate the habit of giving to those who do not have.

I hope I am doing a good job of raising a daughter who knows not to glory in vanity, and that it is a duty to give back. Not only that, but that value for the humanity in others is evidenced by the respect accorded to everyone she meets on a daily basis—be it young, old, poor, rich, black or white.

My life journey has been inspired by beautiful memories of my childhood. I felt loved and valued, and I had a voice. That was very important. There was no limitation set by family values and standards, and being a girl child was not an issue at all. Sport was a major part of our family life. Every one of the children was involved and thrived in one sport or the other. There was life around a tennis table, which was the family's favourite, and my brother was a local champion at it. We all learnt to play, and we all excelled in athletics.

My passion for football (as an ardent Italian SERIE A spectator at the time) developed wings from there, and it led to me being nicknamed 'Bebeto' by male friends from secondary school days. There was no limitations, and I had the freedom to explore and spread my wings. There was no trust deficit on both sides.

I am inspired by knowledge and stories. My mom and dad told a lot of stories, and I tell my daughter lots of stories too. They are unthreatening ways of conveying truths. I hope she has been inspired by my personal life stories and that of others that I have shared with her. I have had to be vulnerable with her and I hope it has been well worth it.

I am inspired by faith and hope. I have always believed there is no alternative, and to not have faith is to lose all sense of inhibition. To not have hope is to die. Faith and hope keeps me sane, and they have come through for me many times. I sell this to my daughter also, and I hope she buys it because she will need lots of it in her generation. Her world seem to resist all the values I am trying to imbibe in her, and she has to contend with greater promotion of falsehood than integrity. She may have to suffer some setbacks if she chooses to fully embrace the values she is being raised with. In those moments of backlash against her values; when her spirit is hurt and in despair, she will need to be inspired by faith and hope. She has to trust that "hope maketh not ashamed". In other words, faith and hope will not fall her hand.

## DAUGHTER

Obedience, respect and honesty are the three major values that I've learnt from home. Naturally, without those values,

I would probably be very carefree about life. But I am accustomed to living by them, so I find myself consciously acting according to those values.

In school, I do see young people placing premium on values the same way I do. Not everyone though, but a lot of people do. The thing is, I think the majority live by the values, not because they want to or understand why they have to, but the fear of their parents is enough to keep them going. It is not as if many young people even have a choice in the matter. It is either they obey or their parents 'skins them alive', according to them.

Staying by the rules hurt sometimes. For one, I am not allowed to sign on to the different social media platforms I would ordinarily want to. I am allowed only a few (boring) ones. My argument is that if I can protect myself, why not let me explore. Many of my friends are on the platforms I want, and their lives are going swell. I am not saying I want to follow my friend's lifestyle or anything, but from my point of view, I think my parents are just over thinking things. Again, there are some values that adults/mothers try to instil that are old-fashioned, like in the area of dressing. Rules about not wearing anything above the knee, or not putting on sleeveless tops, will not go down well with teenagers in this day and age.

The relationship that I have with my mother is one I would choose over some of my friend's, any day, any time. There are definitely some qualities that I wish we could improve in our relationship, but I am not complaining. The truth is that my mom actually instils values in a really good way. She has a way of explaining to me the reason I need to have them and how they could help me overall. Plus, she models the values she sells to me, and so I am fine with going along with it. I think young people should be taught about values, with adults sharing personal and other people's experiences. Without it,

I doubt they would really pay attention to whatever values they are being taught. Young people want to be sure you have been through what they are going through, and that's the only way they know you understand. Then they can easily obtain moral lessons from true life stories, know why they need the values being taught, and as well avoid any bad situation.

Building a relationship with your daughter is definitely the first step to getting her to stick with the values you are teaching her. Some attitudes our mothers put up do not really help the relationship building. Thank God that my mother is not fully washed in the 'Yoruba mother' blood. I know some people whose relationship with their mother is like that of a madam and house help (so you know, in this case the daughter is the house help). In case you don't understand what it means to have a Yoruba mother blood, let me give a brief overview.

- Any bad thing that happens in the house, it is your doing. e.g; when you break something, it is because you are blind and careless, but when your mother breaks it, it is because you didn't place it well in the first place.

- If your mother is talking to you and you are not responding, she will shout and ask you if you are deaf and dumb. When you open your mouth to respond, she will shout, "I am talking and you are talking, Egbami" (meaning, come help me).

- She will call you downstairs and make sure you get there before she tells you to help her get something from upstairs.

- She will also call you downstairs to get something that is about 1cm away from where she is seated.

- She will ask you, "Do you want more (food portion), and

if you make the mistake of answering, "Yes," she will shout, "Come and eat me now".

- She would be more than happy to disgrace you in front of your friends if you have annoyed her.

The above is to stress that communication or instructions from a mother to a daughter needs to be very clear and devoid of shouting. When there is too much sarcasm, insults and blaming, it affects the relationship negatively. When the relationship is affected, communicating value to the child will be very difficult.

I realise that no mother-daughter relationship is perfect, and comparing one's mother or daughter to another can either improve or destroy your relationship, depending on how it is done. When there is something missing from a mother-daughter relationship, we should be able to take tips from other people's relationship; but problem can arise if we are always focused on comparing with others.

I cannot steal, disrespect people, join bad company, do drugs, have premarital sex, etc., because of the values I have been brought up with. I hold them close to my heart and trust them to give me strength to resist the temptation to act in ways that are unbecoming. I do not think I lose opportunities because I hold such strong values. If my values obstruct me from doing or gaining something, then it means it was never a good opportunity (or friendship) in the first place, and I won't have a problem letting it go. I have heard countless stories from my mom about people who have done things that made them go astray, or people with potentials who messed up their lives even before they got a chance to use it; and this helps my viewpoint of life. I know my values are there for a reason, so I cannot just compromise them whenever I want. I do not want to end up like people in the stories I have heard, neither do I want to be a (negative) moral story for other children.

I am inspired by young people around me, who constantly push themselves to stand out. I am inspired by all the legends who have risen above challenging situations to become as legendary as they have become. I am inspired by the opportunities and platforms that I have been given to aspire to my highest potentials. I am inspired to make a difference by the stories of people, especially children, who faced dreadful, preventable experiences that they did not survive. My parents, tutors, and friends, all inspire me to achieve greatness with their words of encouragement. I am constantly surrounded by people who make me believe in myself even when I doubt. I am inspired by great people who walked with God throughout their life's journey, and I wish to do the same.

Usually they say inspiration comes from within, but mine comes from both within and all around me.

# CHAPTER SIX

## THE BOY-FRIEND THINGY

### MOTHER

My confession up front is that my relationship with her father started when I was fourteen (14). It was an innocent friendship, and no mushy-mushy romantic coloration. It was a values-oriented relationship, and we pushed each other to good works. I had many other friends.

Values had always mattered when it came to making friends, including boyfriends. As the saying goes, "Birds of the same feather flock together." It took more than a sweet tongue to 'fall in love' with any boy in the time of my youth (I remind you that I am old school now). The young man had to have something going for him. Either he was top of the class intellectually, had exceptionally good conversational skills, plus manners, or just an adorable saint who went about doing good. Good looks? Blah! It didn't count. Beauty, they say, is in the eye of the beholder. There were many boys who fit the size, and I made many friends. I believe I had more boyfriends than girlfriends. I was comfortable gisting and laughing in their midst. I was one of them. A tomboy. There was no strings attached, and none of my boyfriends extended one. It was all about healthy competition, charging one another up to be the best.

Okay, so I was not Mother Theresa's protégé, and I had my share of crushes along the way. Maybe just one or two. (Her daddy does not count. After all he was a steady friend all through, but he eventually ended up with the prize). I managed it well, I think. Being born-again early on in my youth saw to that. The absolute trust my parents reposed in me was another important check. With all the freedom I was allowed; no restrictions as to where to go or who to see, I was obligated to return the favour. My dad was superb in interacting with all my friends, both boys and girls. They were welcome in our home. One or two boys who visited from out of town even passed the night. Don't get me wrong, there were boys I was crazy about enough to part with some prized possession, like my plate of food, coke, biscuits, and sweets. (What more did a young girl have to give?).

My friendship with boys had no bearing with necking or sex. I knew the limits and the boys knew it too. I did not have to verbalize it. I guess they took a cue from the many moral instruction sessions I had with them (Hic!). I did not even give them the chance to broach the subject. There were boundaries; mine was a very strict one at the time. In preteen/early teenage years, a boy could not even dare place a hand on my shoulder, not even in error. I did not need to slap anyone; the look was killing enough. I soft-pedalled as I grew older. I found that when you grow friendship, and garner deep respect from your peers, including boys, your strict rules about everything is viewed less with scorn. People take you for who you are. The pressure to conform is less, and the potential to influence for good is higher.

Mind you, our personality types play a role in how we start and manage relationships. I was vivacious, very outgoing, and witty. I loved intellectual discussions, and was involved in many debates. I even received an award for 'Most Charismatic' in my undergrad days. I did not need to rebuff unwanted advances with ancestral insults. For some, a witty remark that threw both party into laughter was all it took to regain sanity of the moment. For others, I reasoned with them to see why a lifelong friendship was more beneficial than a relationship going nowhere. A boy asking me out was not a crime, so why would I dent his ego by telling him to hug the electric pole or jump in the lagoon? There is no need to brand any boy a Casanova (do we still use this word in modern day?) just because he asked you out. A boy liking a girl and telling her so does not translate to the boy being a bad person. I am hoping that I have communicated well enough to my daughter that there is always a polite way to decline an offer without making the boy feel like the scum of the earth. No matter the personality type you have been blessed with; never make any boy (or any human being for that matter) feel like shit (literally). It is a rule of thumb.

Oh! There were many things I was naïve about in my time. I took people at face value. I trusted easily. I engaged with others from the place of deep conviction of human kindness. I was proven wrong on some occasions. God's mercy came through for me and shielded me when enemies like friends ensnared me. I acknowledge, however, that I was naïve. I did not see anything wrong in visiting my friend in a private space alone. Shirt pulling, sitting on a boy's lap (or should I say man's lap?), holding hands, pulling cheeks, rough play with physical contacts were activities that seemed okay to me to have with someone I called my friend. I learnt along the way that if that my friend is a boy and he has testosterone, I am better off staying clear of such activities! I hope my darling daughter knows that she can only vouch for her own motives. A girl may hug or play with a guy from a place of friendship and trust, but such an action may communicate something different to a guy. It is better to be safe than assume.

There is that thing about good girls falling in love with bad boys. I don't know about that. It is probably based on the assumption that 'good girls' want some excitement injected into their 'boring' lives. I say again, I don't know about that. I assume I was a 'good girl', but my life was not boring at all. I had the most exciting life without having to be involved in boyfriend/girlfriend drama. As I have told my daughter repeatedly, her daddy was my only 'official boyfriend', and I married him. He was not a 'bad boy' by any standards, and still isn't. Even though I wish he could be the Denzel Washington of my dreams—grow a beard, wear afro, develop six packs, and constantly be in dark shades! I wish.

One thing I know for sure is that values will always be valuable. It is unfortunately too expensive for cheap people thronging all around the place. I did not (and still do not) live by other people's standards. I set my standards, I set my boundaries, and do what is best for me. I learnt to just be my authentic self with everybody; potential boyfriend or not. I think I turned out right. I believe she should take a cue from me.

## DAUGHTER

I cannot fall for a boy at the snap of a finger. It is almost impossible. I do not yet know what a guy could do to steal my affection. I have not given it deep thought before now. Thinking of it now, it would be down to his attitude and personality. When someone has a heart (like a big heart), and demonstrates it in different situations, it speaks well and defies the egoistic nature that the 'male specimen' have been branded with. Like I said, I have not thought deep about it, but I know for sure it goes deeper than handsome looks. He should have a special side.

There are several opinions on the age young girls should be allowed to be in a relationship. Contrary to what the older generation believes, I think there shouldn't really be an 'allowed' age. While not saying that toddlers should be dating, young girls should be allowed to start relationships at any age they deem fit. A relationship is not always as complex as most parents push it out to be; to the extent that they believe you can only start dating at age 25 and above. That is just blahhh. A relationship could just be a bit of a higher level of emotional intimacy that people share, compared to that of their everyday friends. Simple. Teenagers having relationships is nothing new or strange. Many adults had friends who were closer than others in their time. My parents are a case in point. Even if it was more of a friendship, it still started early on. Of course, for teenagers, there has to be a limit, and I think it should be the whole sexual part. When there is a high level of physical intimacy, that sort of crosses the line and may prove 'dangerous'.

Some teenagers have boyfriends because they want to copy their friends, and so feel pressured, but most others just have boyfriends for the fun of it. Honestly, half of teenage relationships are meaningless. They are just for the sake of it. For the sake of having someone closer than others. Someone to boast about to friends. Someone to call 'my boyfriend'. Just that somehow 'different' person.

It is no hidden fact that mothers and daughters usually have conflicts based on boyfriends' issues, and the reason is quite simple: Girl + Boyfriend = Unapproved Relationship = Girl Angry = Mother Daughter Conflict.

I get it, there is always that overprotective factor with mothers. They do not want their daughter to get into any trouble or get hurt. It is just that some mothers do not exactly understand what might be going on, and they just go ahead to exaggerate the whole situation. If at all they want to help their daughters manage their relationships, then they should advise them on their limits, share experiences (truthfully) of how they managed their own relationships at same age, give tips on what to look out for that their daughter might not know about, and then trust them to make wise choices.

My mom is quite alright in how she relates with my friends. Well, considering I attend an all-girls school, it is not like she knows or engages much with my guy friends. But I know that a lot of mothers (of my friends to be exact) have huge problems relating with their daughter's guy friends. They don't even want their daughters to relate with boys in the first instance, and when they eventually meet the guy (or guys), things do not go down well. I wish I knew what goes on in their heads in situations where they see their daughters with a boy. Whether they sincerely do not know what to say, or they choose to get all defensive on purpose, I really do not know. A simple "hi" or "hello", "how are you doing", would be fine, and then you can end the conversation there. No need for jokes (eyes rolling). Please, that is just the worst approach because it creates an awkward atmosphere where the joke is never funny, but my poor guy friend would be forced to laugh.

The story I heard about how my parents met was actually quite nice to hear (at least at first until I heard it a thousand more times!). I liked the fact that their relationship had morals and standards. It was a very good friendship at their early age, before it blossomed into a serious relationship. Frankly, I felt it was too serious with little romance in between (either that or they chose to leave out the juicy details). I could tell there were nice memories because it really sounded like it. Believe it or not, young people in this generation want to create such beautiful memories too.

For me, I am definitely, most certainly not the type to believe in love at first sight or marry my childhood crush. It is too cliché and senseless to me. Why should you be hoping to marry your childhood crush at that stage? Who is even thinking of marriage at that age?! Just maybe there is a tendency if you guys keep in touch, but not that you plan for it. Love at first sight is a phenomenon I still don't understand. How do you see someone for the first time and just 'love' the person? That is a bit queer. Come on! Yes, you can be insanely attracted to the person if he or she is cute. But really, do you immediately get shot with a cupid arrow and you are in love? Naahhh. I don't see how that works. I believe it takes actually knowing somebody to fall in love.

I am perfectly aware that not all boys can be trusted. In fact, I generally have a hard time trusting them. I do not listen to 'charming' words or stuff like that because I am not really affected by them. I know what is right and what is wrong, and cannot be moved by sweet words. I judge each situation and decide for myself what to do so that I can keep myself away from trouble with boys.

People do advise girls that they should always keep their mom posted on everything going on in their life, but I believe there is an extent to that. I would never tell my mom about my interest in any guy (at least not now) because, come on, what do I expect her to say? I can differentiate between an American movie and a Nigerian household. Even the thought of my mom pretending to care and asking, "Oh, what is his name? Is he… blah blah blah," is pretty odd and weird. In fact, she would be more like, "Don't be bothering yourself with boys, focus on your studies… blah blah," and that is obviously not what I would be looking to hear. That is even for my mom who I consider to be a bit liberal. Other girls' attempt to share such thought may be met with a slap, and complemented with mountain of insults. So, I would rather just happily discuss with my friends at this stage. (No offense mom, XOXO).

The whole thing of good girls liking bad boys is cliché or at best, half-true. I think the attraction exists because they are exact opposites. Opposites are said to attract, right? The truth is that bad boys are actually quite exciting and adventurous, as well as dangerous, but some girls would rather ignore the latter. As stereotypical as it sounds, bad boys are actually hot and exhibit confidence, which girls find attractive. Good girls also believe that for some reasons, they can change them, and that's usually where they fall. They fail to realise that they can't change him unless he wants to change.

In all, I would rather my mom relates with me on the basis of trust when it comes to relationships with people generally, and boys in particular, because it would get annoying if she continues asking me questions from time to time, and give me the idea that she has no trust in me.

# CHAPTER SEVEN

## NAVIGATING THE PAIN VALLEYS

### MOTHER

To say that life is full of ups and downs is an understatement. The pain valleys are real, and not even a child is spared. The pain of loss of a loved one; the pain of being cheated and not being able to do anything about it; the pain from trusted friends who turned out to be backstabbers; the pain of being mistreated and abused by family members; the pain from sexual abuse; the pain from losing an opportunity; the pain from despair, depression and despondency. I wish we could wish them away. But anyway, our hearts and mind must be prepared to deal with them.

On my journey to where I am today, I have witnessed many wickedness. Example, man's inhumanity to man. I carried the hurt of friends who had to bear the pain of parental rejection at tender ages. Absentee fathers who escaped responsibility for their actions by denying the paternity of a child. They do not understand the pain they put a child through; a child who grows up to feel s/he is unlovable. Parents going through the pain of separation/divorce, putting their child or children in the middle as a bargaining chip. As if it is not bad enough that a child has to deal with choosing which parent to move in with, s/he has to listen to each parent bad mouth the other in order to gain some leverage. Adults laying their own burden on the shoulder of a child.

Then there were the scenarios of families who had everything going for them—well-paying jobs, a comfortable home, good schools for the children, and impeccable social standing. Suddenly, they lost everything. No job, no comfortable home to live in anymore. They are at the mercy of neighbours and families to assure a day's meal. The children drop out from high-end schools and enroll in public schools. The opportunity to make something out of their lives seem to have faded into oblivion.

I saw the pain of the loss. I witnessed first-hand the meaning of the phrase "No condition is permanent". They were my friends.

Some friends and acquaintances lost parents, in some cases, both parents on the same day. That pain could only have been imagined. The impact on their academic pursuit was huge. Some had to say goodbye to old friends and move in with relatives far away from familiar terrain. Not all of these stories ended well. While some of the children in these stories literally made lemonades out of the lemons life served them, others fell flat on their faces and made a bad situation even worse.

I was not spared my own share of pain growing up. As an active preteen who was in the school relay team, leading the school choral group, leading the debating club, and generally up and about, to be side lined by a debilitating illness that took me away from school for almost two school terms, the pain can only be better imagined. The pain from illness is one thing, the pain of missing out on the things you considered paramount to your existence is another. To my young mind then, I just wanted to be back in school with my friends. And yes, I got back to school and still beat my friends to the top position in the class (my friends still talk about this till date). There were however other things I had to let go for life. I mean for life. No more track and field! Not just that, I had to deal with being different in high school. Considering I used a walking stick for the better part of six years, I was not very invisible. Being in and out of hospital for many years was tough; letting go of many dreams as a result of ill-health was painful, but I learnt perspective along the way. I learnt that life deals us different hands, and we have to be thankful for what we have going well for us. I learnt that when we think deeply about it or look around us, we may have been dealt a better blow than others; our case is not necessarily the worst. I learnt that tough times never last, but tough people do. I learnt that life is what we make of it; we could either allow the pain to build character in us or allow it destroy our self-esteem and our access to all the beauty life has to offer. It is a choice.

I have had a full life in spite of the many challenges. In fact, I can say I have had a ball. Life as a teenager was not boring at all. I made the most of activities I could be involved in. I had the best of friends. My friends had their share of pain, loss, disillusionment, abuse, lack, and what have you, but all that only served to bind us. We were determined to be the best academically, and we stuck to that common goal.

My mom was priceless through all of my pain. A mother carries her child's pain just as if it was hers. She had all of her plans rearranged to fit the very many hospital visits, therapy and all. She had worries written all over her face many times, and I witnessed her cry in anguish, not once or twice, with the hand life had dealt her. Still she remained resolute in providing all the support I needed, while making out time to care for my four siblings who needed her just as much.

The support from home made it easier to navigate the

valley of pain. A mother's love, thoughtfulness, kind words, and prayers, made the world seem bright rather than bleak. She exemplified what it means to push on even when you feel your back cannot bend forward more than it already has. And it was good training as I also learnt to carry the burden of raising a special needs child without buckling under the weight.

Life is definitely not a bed of roses. I hope my daughter recognises this, and is prepared to face life's battles with courage. I have shared my story with her, and the story of countless others. Not just the story of pain and gloom, but of amazons rising above the ashes. I hope I have successfully communicated to her that I have her back through thick and thin; in good times and in bad. I hope she understands that we are allowed to fall many times, but not allowed to remain down and defeated. Even if she were to make the biggest mistake of her life, her mother is there to support her as she navigates whatever valley of pain life deals her.

## DAUGHTER

Pain, if I may say so, is an everyday thing. Several things cause young people pain. I don't mean just physical pain, there are emotional pains too. The pain comes to different persons in different ways. Some people get pained when their emotional needs are not tended to; needs like love, care, attention, happiness, etc. Shame, embarrassment, disappointment and harm also have a way of causing young people pain.

I have had my little share of painful experiences. Mostly when I was younger, I always had these horrible thoughts and dreams and they always caused me pain. Such days, I mostly went to bed crying because I kept thinking that I was going to die any moment. My mom knew it was all in my imagination, and found a way to help me deal with it. My point is that most of my pain came from fear. Fear of not looking a particular way, or of not achieving something. Basically, fear had its hold on me.

The common painful experiences I see young people go through has do to with rejection/acceptance, hurtful words, family issues, shame and things like that. Young people are always seeking acceptance in one form or the other. When rejection comes, it is like a blow to the chest; whether it is in a relationship or a group of friends or an important other. Betrayal also brings pain, and it is very common among young people. For some, trust is easy, but for others, it is a difficult task. When you do eventually trust someone, and the person goes on to betray you, it hurts a lot. Whether the person was close to you or not, the fact that your trust was broken is really painful.

There are some of my friends that have family issues, and even though they try to mask it, the pain is still visible in their actions. When young people have it bad at home and channel that pain through angry outbursts or misbehaviours, we are quick to judge them, but what they are going through kind of accounts for their actions or inactions.

Embarrassment and shame is another agonising experience for teenagers because fellow teenagers can be innocently vicious. They make it such that the embarrassing experience would haunt you for a long time; they would help it sink in even more. When reference is repeatedly made to the embarrassing experience, it hurts, and hurtful words have one of the most damaging effects on teens. Sometimes people say things jokingly (I admit I am guilty of doing this countless times) without realising the implication, but the thing with these 'innocent' words is that they stick. Nobody likes to hear bad things said about them. Once they do, they sometimes start believing those bad things and then do bad things.

Different people handle pain in different ways, but in general, I don't think young people handle pain well. A lot of young people see painful experiences as God's way of punishing them, and they get back at Him by misbehaving and acting out. It is usually painful experiences that lead young people into making bad decisions because that's the only way they feel they can vent their anger. Some people inflict physical harm to themselves to make the emotional pain go away, but this never really works. The self-harm starts because young people believe they can deal with pain on their own. This is rarely true as it is not exactly easy to do—dealing with pain alone. Young people also inflict physical harm on themselves in order to get attention from older ones about a particular pain they are going through. Sometimes, I deal with my pain by venting to myself, which then either gets me angrier or keeps me calm. I'm aware it is not exactly the best method. I keep exploring the best ways to manage my pain.

If a mother is very observant (which a mother should be), she would notice when her daughter is hurt. One thing I realise is that teens are champions when it comes to bottling things up on the inside, and sometimes don't know who exactly to let it out to. But when they do, damn! It is like the best feeling one could have. Mothers should really push their children to talk most of the time. And when I say push their children to talk, I don't mean the type when they say, "Dear, are you okay?" and take the "no" that they are most likely to get for an answer. They could help their daughters work out the possible reason for the negative emotion; suggest possible cause of the hurt they are feeling until they talk. If they are so adamant on keeping quiet, at least assure them that they have somebody to talk to. Sometimes young people are not okay to share their pains with their mother, either because of the type of issue causing the pain or the level of relationship they have with their mother. However, if the inability to share the pain is because of a lack of quality relationship, then the moms should find how to fix it. I personally can and do share some of my painful experiences with my mom. Some. I would be reluctant if I brought the cause of the pain upon myself, but if I'm at the edge where I really need someone to talk to, then, I would have no choice but to share with her. Talking through, from my point of view, is the best way a mother can support her daughter to manage pain.

Listening to or reading about people who have gone through way worse experiences with pain than I have, can encourage me to go through the valley of pain and remain strong. I've listened to countless stories of people who went through very terrible experiences, and still came out strong. So I am reassured that if such people (even some my age) can face their pain and rise above it, then what little thing am I going through that I cannot get out of? I have never experienced the pain of the death of someone or people really close to me, and to be honest, that is a kind of pain that I am constantly afraid that I might not be able to rise above. It even hurts thinking about it, because, for my kind of person, I am not really sure how I would get past it.

I don't really think that young people are adequately prepared to deal with the many painful experiences and challenges that life can bring. I realise that most of the time, our parents don't prepare us for them. They probably think they are trying to 'protect' us when they are just postponing the painful reality. When painful circumstances eventually come, some parents don't really have a starting point to engage their teen (s). It is harder at that stage to make their hurt teen take comfort in any words they say. We need to know, and we can't if adults don't tell us the difficulties going on around us. Mothers have a responsibility to prep their daughters on life situations beforehand, in different ways that suites each person, just as long as the message is passed across. This way, it is easier for teenagers to deal with these situations when they happen, and not resort to drugs, gangs, prostitution, or any other rash way of dealing with their pain.

# CHAPTER EIGHT

## DISCIPLINE VERSUS PUNISHMENT

### MOTHER

To cane or not to cane? This is the debate that has been ongoing for years. The debate has been louder in this generation in the light of many cases of abuse at home, in school and other places of interest. I do not believe in the cane. I have had my reservations about the use of cane from way back when it was very popular. I cannot actually remember being flogged by my parents. It might have happened, but it could only have been on very few occasions for me not to remember. There were the popular 'Igbati' (slap), 'Iko' (knock on the head), and the repeated threat of getting the belt. If I did not get my ass whooped to the point where I could remember it, it means my parents adopted alternative ways of getting across to my sense of responsibility. I decided way back that I would try their approach in raising my own children.

There are definitely many things that are irksome to a mother. Consider scenarios where your daughter refuses a particular meal or a particular dress. There were many times I have been beside myself with anger. The first thought that comes to mind is to show this little madam who is boss around here. There were times when she was a little girl that I had wielded the stick out of frustration. To hear her come back with statements like, "Beat me as much as you like," in a defiant way showed me I was on the wrong path.

For a long time now, I have attended to the issue of setting standards by disciplining and not punishing. I recognise there is a difference. While punishment is used to control a child's behaviour, discipline is meant to develop the child's behaviour. I desire to see my daughter decipher what is the best behaviour to adopt per time; learn self-control without diminishing her self-confidence. I purposed early on to discuss the rules, and have both of us agree on what is acceptable, and what is not. I find that it is less stressful for me to adopt the style of reward and praise rather than reacting to misbehaviour. The thought of raising the stick alone weakens every tendon in my arms. I lack energy to cane. I would rather talk, give her the benefit of doubt that she has a brain that functions well enough to understand the ABC of why she should do some things, and why she should not do some other things.

Never mind the fact that I flew off the handle many times, especially on things that border on cleaning up in the kitchen, tidying the room, completing an assignment within the timeframe given, or losing items and having a laissez faire attitude to it. My blood boils, but in my estimate, the wielding of the cane would not solve anything. I chastise; but with words of mouth. I am saved the strain to my upper right hand shoulder which hurts already from constant typing on the computer!

Truth be told, I second guess myself many times as to whether my approach is the best possible one. With parenting, you never know; you keep trying your best. I have not seen anything to make me alarmed. I reckon that if discipline, as against punishment, worked for me, it would work for my little girl. I do not want her to adopt good behaviour just so as to avoid punishment. I want her to see how priceless her life is, and appreciate how 'good' behaviour enhances her value before God and before man. I am quick to note that some things that are considered 'good behaviour' in my generation may not be given the same value in hers. In my generation, when an older person gives a directive, you immediately follow instructions without questioning. Now, the question 'why?' is a quick counter to any directive given to young people. In my generation, when our parents fart, especially when we are all watching the TV, you pretend nothing happened. Not after you have been repeatedly brainwashed that the fart from an adult 'does not smell'. In her generation, they will call the adult out immediately, no matter how old. It is the age of child rights and child participation after all.

## DAUGHTER

Self-discipline is knowing how to act and behave without being told; or teaching yourself what to do, and the right time to do it. Self-discipline is what we are expected to aim for so as to reduce the punishment that comes from our parents. We get it.

Obviously, young people hate discipline in the form of punishment. The use of cane feels quite cruel to young people in general, although some are used to it. Some people dread the use of cane on them after they have misbehaved. A lot of teenagers will consciously misbehave, already counting the strokes of cane they would receive. They don't feel threatened by the cane (anymore). Some honestly love their cane (and you have no idea how much). These ones have been beaten to the extent that they feel nothing anymore, and even look forward to the exhilarating rush that comes with beating. Some others fear the cane with their life, or any punishment at all, that they would happily steer away from bad behaviour.

For me, if my mom needs to correct me, I would rather

her just tell me what needs to be said in a calm way. That way, I can listen and understand where she is coming from. Spanking and shouting don't really work for me. Not that my mom spanks me, but I am just saying. Shouting, oftentimes, gives me a tendency to blank out while my mom is ranting away. This is not exactly deliberate, it is just my way of coping with what is going on.

Painful punishments may widen the gap in the relationship between a mother and her daughter (or worsen an already bad relationship). One thing is sure, young people hate punishments; so if a mother punishes her daughter in a mean way, or in a way that hurts her, it would definitely affect their relationship negatively; especially if the girl becomes scared. It hurts even more when young people do not understand exactly what they have done wrong. Truth is, many adults have different ideas of what is right or wrong, as compared to how teens view it. For example, adults believe that young people 'talking back' to an adult is wrong, but most times, it is just us trying to express our point of view. There is like a really long list of things adults believe are acts of indiscipline to which teens have a contrary view. For instance, also, people believe chewing gum is a sign of indiscipline, but I don't really see the correlation.

The discipline experience for me at home has been completely normal. For one, my parents don't beat me (except for the one or two swipes I received from my dad when I was much younger). It has never been a disciplinary method. My parents talk to me, tell me what I did wrong when they need to. I am not troublesome anyway, so that doesn't really happen often. Other (few) times, they might decide to take away privileges like going out and stuff like that.

My mom is not always overbearing with the standards she sets. As regards disciplinary standards, the level she sets is quite okay. Maybe there are just a few that I disagree with, especially on days when she takes the totalitarian stance. I get annoyed when I meet up to standard, and I'm not commended for it. But when I falter, I get reprimanded. Times like that, I couldn't really be bothered about whatever standards I'm expected to follow. I think mothers should let the commendations be louder than the reprimands.

# CHAPTER NINE

## GRATITUDE MODE

### MOTHER

Motherhood does not come with a manual. We learn through the socialization process, asking questions and opening our googly eyes in observation. I often say that it is important to learn from those who have run the race ahead of you. Identify the potholes or ditches they fell into, and refrain from doing same. I know it is easier said than done, but making effort is a good starting point.

Playing mom to my beautiful daughter has not been a walk in the park. It has and is taking a lot of personal reflections, building my repertoire of information, and adjusting perceptions as we go along. There have been many more highs than lows, and I count my blessings many times for giving me a daughter I am so proud of.

I am grateful for the privilege of being a mother in the first instance. To get married, conceive, and have a live birth is not 'normal'. I attribute it to the special grace and mercies of God who has a plan for us from the foundations of the earth. I'm grateful that she came first before her brother, because she has played second mommy very well in the last ten years. To have a daughter who visibly loves her sibling, despite his many 'troubles', is worthy of thanksgiving. We do know of families who have to grapple with sibling's rivalry gone out of control. In the many years where I had to deal with the brother's special needs, she was my very able deputy carer. Even though she had to let go of many things to accommodate her brother's tantrums, she was not bitter or hurtful towards him. It takes an angel to be and act like that.

I am grateful for her strong mind, but gentle disposition. So much so that she earned the title 'Small, but Mighty' in her primary school days. Memories flood my mind of her toddler days when she would dance, sing and have no cares in the world. She was not one to deny anyone her toys. She was and still is a very giving person. Her strong will has stood her out in her academic pursuit. She does not need to be followed up to sit at the reading table. She is mature enough to prioritize time for play and time for study. She has made me proud many times. Her academic feat would make any mother proud.

We have had our share of fights, but which mother and daughter haven't? It has never stopped my appreciation of how obedient she is, even when she is not in total agreement with my instructions. And how I love the fact that she does not take for granted her access to things belonging to me or the family as a whole. She would ask to pick a bottle of drink from the fridge, ask if she could use my scarf, ask to make a call on my phone, or even ask if she could have a second helping of chicken. Those are endearing qualities I am grateful for.

Oh, how I laugh when she starts her silly dance, or when she rolls her eyes at my attempt to act funky. The knowing look and burst of laughter at someone's unsuccessful attempt to look trendy. The priceless moments under the duvet when we would have girl talk, or times when we would band against her brother and her father just for the fun of it.

She is evolving; she is growing into her own. We do not

agree on everything. I keep my eyes wide open even as I try to respect her privacy. I remind her that I trust her, and hope she does not betray my trust. I still tell her plenty stories; mine and those of others, and I trust that the stories make a difference.

Above all, I pray for her that she will fulfil her destiny. I remind myself that she is not me, and I cannot shape her to be what she is not. I therefore hand her over to God who predestined her and equipped her for the work she is to do on this earth. There are many things I hope and wish for her; such as abiding in God's love, be full of peace and happiness, be fulfilled in the works of her hands, and that she will suffer no heartbreaks (A mother has a right to wish this, right?).

I am learning to focus on all the beautiful things going for us and be grateful. I am counting my very many blessings as regards my daughter, and naming them one by one. I am equally grateful that my mother made all of the sacrifices she made to get me here. The least I can do is to cheer my own daughter on.

Bravo Girl! Let's go take the world by storm.

## DAUGHTER

I am grateful for many things actually. I'm grateful for my parents. I am grateful for my family members. I am grateful for God's grace and goodness. I am grateful for the things that my parents can provide for me. I am grateful for every waking day. I am grateful that I am whole, hearty and constantly protected. I am grateful for academic success. I am grateful for the many opportunities I have that many do not have access to. Most of all, I am grateful that I have too many things to be grateful for.

There are too many memories that will remain with me

from childhood, and I would have to dedicate another book to writing them all if I had to. I remember the times when I would pull up my long skirt all the way to my chest (make it look like a dress), put on my mom's oversized shades and finish off my signature look with my famous Barbie glass plastic heels (it literally came from a Barbie pack, and yes, my feet were that small). I remember the teary moment when I walked down the aisle (as a flower girl of course) at my uncle's wedding. The time I cried for over thirty minutes because I was refused more portion of food. I remember all my primary school experiences and milestones such as graduation. I remember my first date with my dad after graduation. I remember being mortified and afraid when I had to give a speech in front of a crowd.

I remember the times when I was younger. My mom wasn't always around because she had to work out of town for a long period (and for the good of the family). I remember always being so joyful to get back from school and see my mom there, waiting. I always looked forward to it because she never failed to play with us and always kept us occupied. I remember another time when my dad had spanked me because I kept pushing his buttons when he had asked me to do something. I had cried like my life depended on it, and being my hero, my mom comforted me till I was okay. I would always cherish the times when we would just lie together on the bed to talk and laugh (...recall the sexuality story) and gist about different things. She would share her thoughts on issues bothering me, and give advice when I needed it, especially as I grew older. These are moments that I will always remember.

Even if most times I do not voice it out or show it, I am and will always be most grateful for all the sacrifices that my mother has to constantly make on my behalf. Sometimes it leaves me feeling so selfish that she has to give up her leisure and do a lot of stressful things just to keep us happy. I couldn't be more grateful to her for that. She is always constantly working her butt off to provide stuff that would eventually not even benefit her. The love that she shows towards my brother and I is just absolutely amazing. Honestly, even if I get angry over the stupidest things sometimes, I know deep in my gut that God could not have given me a better mother.

Like any normal person, I wish to be extremely successful. I wish to accomplish all my goals and aspirations. I wish to make a difference in the lives of people around me and the world at large. I hope that I would be able to give back to my parents and my community in the future or even now. I wish to bring a smile on people's faces. I wish to be happy.

# EPILOGUE

What we have attempted to do in this book is to share our journey with you. Yes, it is a never ending journey. We only know the end results we desire, but not necessarily the vehicle and the roads that we will need to travel to get there. We just want our individual aspirations and the expectations we have of each other to come to fruition.

Our aim is to get mothers and their teenage daughters mostly to start having conversations that would help strengthen their relationship. We recognize there are many factors that impact this relationship, and the factors are not the same for all families. There are different factors like personality types, socio-economic status, family dynamics, religious beliefs/values, etc., that will certainly inform the way mothers and daughters approach the issues discussed in this book. It will also affect how heated the conflicts between them will be, and how the conflicts will be resolved. Notwithstanding these factors, we are certain a respectful and honest communication will give mothers and daughters the best chance at negotiating these inevitable issues, while maintaining an overall healthy and loving relationship. This will not only ensure a safer ride on your own journey, but would hopefully strengthen the bond between you and your daughter. This is our goal.

So, this is not a manual; it is a conversation starter.

We hope this checklist, on issues raised in each chapter of the book, would draw attention to areas for reflection and engagement for both daughter and mother. Mother and daughter can use the checklist at individual levels and/or jointly (preferably) to assess what they are doing well or where they are doing poorly in their mother-daughter relationship. An honest conversation, with an open mind from both is recommended. In some cases, it would be a difficult conversation to have. This assessment may take place over a period of time, long enough to address all the knotty issues.

After each period of assessment, they could set out an action plan to enable them do better in relevant areas of reflection. Such actions could include but not limited to:

- Buy books on parenting a teenager

- Agree with daughter on a day dedicated to 'mother-daughter bonding'

- Start sexuality conversations with daughter

- Buy a 'Thank You' card for mother, or write 'Thank You' notes frequently

- Seek external (to family) mediation in mother-daughter protracted conflict situation

- Start meeting of a small group of mothers who become support systems and accountable to one another on issues raised in this book

- Daughter reduces hanging out with friends and prioritizes her education

- Mother starts some skills development/personal development programs to enhance personal value.

As opportunity and time presents, we hope to convene meet-ups where mothers and daughters can have live, rich conversations along the lines of topics in this book and much more.

Wishing you the best life has to offer.


A toast to every mother and daughter out there!

# CONVERSATION STARTER: CHECKLIST

## Chapter One: Friends and Foes

\_\_\_\_ Mother dislikes or is critical of daughter's friends

\_\_\_\_ Mother is pushing daughter towards friendship with particular persons/family

\_\_\_\_ Mother is anxious daughter makes friends too quickly and too many

\_\_\_\_ Mother is anxious daughter is anti-social; not making efforts to make friends

\_\_\_\_ Daughter thinks mother is too intrusive in her friendships

\_\_\_\_ Daughter feels mother is rude to her friends

\_\_\_\_ Daughter dislikes her mother's friends

\_\_\_\_ Daughter thinks mother sees enemies everywhere too often

# Chapter Two: Body Image and Fashion

____ Mother does not understand why daughter is so self-conscious

____ Mother is concerned about daughter's weight gain from eating too much

____ Mother insists on picking out clothes for daughter

____ Mother pays daughter compliments every time she is dressed up

____ Mother discusses clothes choices with daughter

____ Mother is afraid of daughter's obsession with skinny look

____ Mother fears daughter dresses like a tomboy

____ Mother worries that daughter is pressured by friends to look and dress in a certain way

____ Daughter thinks mother is too obsessed about fashion and body image

____ Daughter fears mother is trying to make her look 'hot and sexy'

____ Daughter is embarrassed by mother's fashion sense

____ Daughter compliments mother's look from time to time

____ Daughter asks mother's opinion on clothes choices

____ Daughter spends too much time looking at fashion magazines and models

____ Daughter wears mother's clothes/shoes without permission

____ Daughter is stealing money to buy fashion accessories

____ Daughter is hiding certain clothes and accessories from mother

____ Daughter is not happy about mother's snide remarks at her look

# Chapter Three: Spiritual Matters

\_\_\_\_ Mother worries that daughter is not taking a serious stance on spiritual matters

\_\_\_\_ Mother has conflicts with daughter using curse words

\_\_\_\_ Mother is concerned that daughter carries practice of religion overboard

\_\_\_\_ Mother feels daughter is disrespectful of spiritual authority figures

\_\_\_\_ Mother makes out time to talk with daughter about spiritual matters

\_\_\_\_ Daughter does not enjoy the spiritual talk with mother because it sounds like being forced to accept

\_\_\_\_ Daughter likes a moderate form of religious practice

\_\_\_\_ Daughter likes an extreme form of religious practice

\_\_\_\_ Daughter does not think her lifestyle negates her religious beliefs

\_\_\_\_ Daughter is not interested in attending religious gatherings

\_\_\_\_ Daughter feels mother's attitude/behaviour is at variance with the religious belief she professes

\_\_\_\_ Daughter argues with mother on yardstick for measuring a religious girl

## Chapter Four: Of Predators and Deceivers

\_\_\_\_ Mother often talks to daughter about challenges of predators and deceivers

\_\_\_\_ Mother has had sexuality talk with daughter

\_\_\_\_ Mother does not know how to initiate sexuality discussion with daughter

\_\_\_\_ Mother shares her own sexuality experiences and general lessons with daughter from time to time

\_\_\_\_ Mother is concerned about daughter's lifestyle, even after talk on predators

\_\_\_\_ Mother worries about daughter's time spent on the internet and picture posting

\_\_\_\_ Mother is concerned that daughter's dressing may expose her to abuse

\_\_\_\_ Mother has exposed daughter to skills for preventing and mitigating exposure to any form of abuse (self-defence)

\_\_\_\_ Mother is concerned abused daughter is taking too long to move on

\_\_\_\_ Mother feels daughter has not learnt her lessons from previous abuse

\_\_\_\_ Daughter does not enjoy sexuality talk from mother; sounds like threat

\_\_\_\_ Daughter does not like uncles and aunts living with them

\_\_\_\_ Daughter is afraid to share with mother a sexual or emotional threat or challenge that she is currently experiencing at home, in school, or in the neighbourhood

____ Daughter feels mother is abusive

____ Abused daughter feels mother does not understand her emotional needs

# Chapter Five: Values and Inspiration

____ Mother is not happy about daughter's character traits at the moment

____ Mother emphasises acceptable values to daughter in words and action

____ Mother feels daughter is being influenced negatively by friends

____ Mother exemplifies to daughter that she can cheat her way through anything

____ Mother clarifies values with daughter in a non-criticising manner

____ Mother uses personal life experiences to teach values to daughter

____ Daughter does not feel inspired by mother

____ Daughter thinks mother is too hard and her rules too stringent

____ Daughter does not feel her mother loves or cares about her

____ Daughter does not feel mother practices what she preaches about values

____ Daughter enjoys every aspect of the relationship with mother

____ Daughter makes statements that seem to appreciate friends' mother's way of life as compared to her mother's

____ Daughter likes some things about mother's values but dislikes some others

___ Daughter holds values learnt from mother very close to heart

## Chapter Six: The Boyfriend Thingy

____ Mother likes what she sees so far with daughter's interaction with boys

____ Mother is not sure how to broach the subject of daughter's interest in boys

____ Mother thinks daughter has too many male friends hanging around

____ Mother has had conversations with daughter about dating and limits

____ Mother shares with daughter personal life stories on boy/male friends

____ Mother feels daughter is too emotional and cannot manage boyfriends now

____ Mother is concerned daughter believes too much in fairy tale love stories

____ Mother is worried that daughter has X-rated movies on her devices

____ Daughter does not like mother sneaking into her private business

____ Daughter can tell mother everything relating to her interest in a boy

____ Daughter believes mother just does not get her views about boys

____ Daughter is not comfortable with how mother interacts with her guy friends

____ Daughter does not see anything wrong in necking and having sex with a boy

____ Daughter wants mother to trust her to do the right things as regards boys

____ Daughter not happy that mother has many male friends who call or visit

____ Daughter does not feel mother has the moral right to caution her about boys

# Chapter Seven: Navigating the Pain Valleys

____ Mother is not sure how to start the subject of pain and loss with daughter

____ Mother has been vulnerable; shared stories of pain/heartbreaks with daughter

____ Mother feels daughter is insensitive to her emotional needs, for instance, following divorce, loss of a loved one, disappointments, etc.

____ Mother looks out for signs that daughter is in any kind of pain

____ Mother talks with daughter through her pain and never accepts brush-offs

____ Mother tells daughter how much she loves her even when she messes up

____ Mother projects her fears and hurts to her daughter

____ Mother seeks professional help for her pain and that of her daughter when necessary

____ Mother knows what to do to help herself and her daughter in the event of rape

____ Daughter feels mother is still carrying the weight of the pain life has dealt her

____ Daughter believes mother is not truthful about her past

____ Daughter wishes she could share her pain with her mother

____ Daughter enjoys being able to ask mother anything about her past or life

\_\_\_\_ Daughter is acting out, and mother feels she has lost control

\_\_\_\_ Daughter is not sharing pain with mother; afraid of being thought of as childish

\_\_\_\_ Daughter not sharing pain with mother; afraid of rebuffs or rejections

\_\_\_\_ Daughter just wants to cry and have her mother hold her and console her

\_\_\_\_ Daughter feels hurt about parent's separation and mother's neglect of her needs

# Chapter Eight: Discipline versus Punishment

____ Mother has no problem using the cane on her daughter

____ Mother believes she is focused on discipline and not just expressing her frustration at her daughter's behaviour

____ Mother has had talks with daughter on rules of engagement and expectations

____ Mother explains to daughter the reasons for rules

____ Mother praises or rewards daughter for good behaviour

____ Mother is overwhelmed by daughter's misbehaviour

____ Daughter thinks mother is not fair in the rules/standards she sets

____ Daughter sees mother as a role model she does not want to disappoint

____ Daughter does not feel appreciated enough for the efforts she makes

____ Daughter feels mother is just being abusive and not instilling discipline

____ Daughter thinks mother hurls hurtful words in the bid to enforce discipline

____ Daughter does not feel mother has moral right to enforce discipline

____ Daughter feels mother expects perfection and does not give her a break

# Chapter Nine: Gratitude Mode

____ Mother often expresses gratitude for many things in daughter's presence

____ Mother knows she is responsible for building the relationship between herself and her daughter

____ Mother teaches daughter to be grateful through story-sharing

____ Mother tells daughter often how blessed she is to have her

____ Mother feels daughter does not show appreciation for whatever she gets

____ Mother prays for and with her daughter

____ Daughter is grateful for mother and her many sacrifices

____ Daughter expresses love and appreciation to mother from time to time

____ Daughter does not feel appreciated by the mother

____ Daughter has no good memories to reflect on growing up with mother

____ Daughter knows she is as responsible as her mother in building a mutually beneficial mother-daughter relationship

www.ingramcontent.com/pod-product-compliance
Lightning Source LLC
Chambersburg PA
CBHW051348040426
42453CB00007B/465